MAUREEN DUFFY was born in 1933 in Worthing, Sussex. As well as being a poet, playwright and novelist, she has also published biographies of Aphra Behn and Henry Purcell, and *The Erotic World of Faery*, a book-length study of eroticism in faery fantasy literature.

After a tough childhood, Duffy took her degree in English from King's College London. She went on to be a teacher from 1956 to 1961, and edited three editions of a poetry magazine called *The Sixties*. She then turned to writing full-time as a poet and playwright after being commissioned to produce a screenplay by Granada Television. In 1960 her play, *Pearson*, won the City of London Young Playwrights Award. She made her début as a novelist with *That's How It Was*, published to wide acclaim in 1962. Her first openly gay novel was *The Microcosm* (1966), set in the famous Gateways Club in London. Among her later novels, *Gor Saga* was televised in 1988 in a three-part mini-series called *First Born*, starring Charles Dance, the London trilogy of *Wounds*, *Capital* and *Londoners* are now available in ebook form, and her latest publications are the poetry collection *Family Values* (Enitharmon Press, 2008) and a novel *The Orpheus Trail* (Arcadia, 2009). She is also the author of 16 plays for stage, television and radio, the most recent being *Sappho Singing* in 2010. A new novel, *In Times Like These*, will also be published by Arcadia.

Duffy has published 31 books, including six volumes of poetry. Her *Collected Poems, 1949–84* appeared in 1985. Her work has often used Freudian ideas and Greek myth as a framework.

She took an active part during the debates around homosexual law reform, which culminated in the Act of 1967. In 1977 she published *The Ballad of the Blasphemy Trial*, a broadside against the trial of the *Gay News* newspaper for 'blasphemous libel'.

She has also been active in a variety of groups representing the interest of writers, and is currently the President of the Authors Licensing and Copyright Society, and a Fellow and Vice President of the Royal Society of Literature. She is deeply interested in issues around enforcing traditional forms of intellectual property law, and is President of the British Copyright Council, and a Fellow of King's College London. She was made a D.Litt. by Loughborough University in 2011 for services to literature and equality law.

Maureen Duffy

Environmental Studies

ENITHARMON PRESS

First published in 2013
by Enitharmon Press
26B Caversham Road
London NW5 2DU

www.enitharmon.co.uk

Distributed in the UK by
Central Books
99 Wallis Road
London E9 5LN

Distributed in the USA and Canada
by Dufour Editions Inc.
PO Box 7, Chester Springs
PA 19425, USA

ISBN: 978-1-907587-28-3

Enitharmon Press gratefully acknowledges the financial support of
Arts Council England, through Grants for the Arts.

British Library Cataloguing-in-Publication Data.
A catalogue record for this book is available
from the British Library.

Designed in Albertina by Libanus Press
and printed in England by SRP

CONTENTS

CRAFTY

You made handbags out of milk bottle tops
bound in raffia; machined rugs out of rags
and odd balls of wool; sewed cami-knickers
from parachute silk, my first satchel
handkerchiefs from flourbags; cooked up bread poultices
sheepshead brawn; crocheted cuffs and collars;
smocked, pleated, piped; cable and moss stitched.
Cakes though weren't your forte. You were defter
unspooling golden syrup onto mounds
of bread and marge, doled out slice by slice
or recycling the weekend's leftovers.

Now, sitting here, turning up trouser legs,
apprentice task, I'm aware that even
the names for your skills are exiting Left
out of my head and the mother tongue.
Shop-soiled, shop-spoiled, we learn to forget.

MAMMICKS

'Obsolete', the dictionary dubs it or, lip curling, 'dialect'.
Cold meat on Monday, shepherded into pie on Tuesday
or sandwiched into my uncle's lunchbox
bubble-and-squeaked on Wednesday with last night's
cold mashed; Thursday was stew or steak-and-kidney
pudding and we were glad to have said
goodbye to the mammicks, a word that came down the line
to start a new life in the smoke for another century.

When I find it again, made classy by Shakespeare
and scholarship, meaning 'cut in little pieces,
leftovers', it still has the tag 'origin obscure'
an old word for old ways now warmed up again
as the cold bites, though the words themselves
buried under fast-food technospeak
like burnt out loves never return.

'WHAT'S FOR TEA?'

Friday was fish night. Not battered and fried
from the chipshop but fresh from Livermore's
in Angel Lane, round the corner from where
Great-aunt Maggie lived with daughters Maudie
and Rose who patted the yellow butter
into shape at The Stores with wooden bats:

saffron cockles with rude black tongues
winkles behind shiny front doors to be
teased out with a skilful pin that could unwind
to their very end, then souse in vinegar and white pepper

brown shrimps armour plated, burnished bloaters
with slippery soft or pinhead hard roes
iridescent mackerel that fed on drowned men's eyes
or a slither of eels with mash and green parsley gravy.

Saturday dinner was the time for fish and chips
wing of skate with whalebone ribs, dogfish
alias rock salmon, rarely dull eyed cod.
So I understand those mussel middens

our forerunners heaped on sea or lake shore
relics of Friday teas, breakfasts and dinners.
'Not fish again!' 'Go out and catch a mammoth then.'
No wonder they were glad to see the Mesolithic
bringing them bread, biscuits, cake
even if it meant harnessing themselves to the plough.

WOODLOUSE

Nanno crustacean, land lobster, you're marooned
in the arctic whiteness of the washbasin.
I try my emergency drill: the plug
with its mountain-rescue chain that usually
works for stranded arachnid or beetle.
How long can you live without food? Water
there is of course, air and china white light.
I put out a tentative forefinger.
Are you dead already, tired, asleep?
You start to run on myriad fine feet
but not towards the rescue hoist of chain.
Shouldn't I just turn the tap and wash you away
put you out of your misery as they say?
Maybe after the gush, the flush, you'd fetch up
on the side of some sewer or septic tank
and clamber out. But I can't risk
that little spark snuffed so I take
a piece of card, life raft or magic carpet
and set it down in your path. You peripatet
forward with my finger urging you on.
I heft you skywards then down to the tiled floor
and you scurry away to the safety of a skirting board.
A small triumph like the bird flung
from cupped hands up into sunlight.

PARAKEETS

Walking the dog today in the gardens
where bishops once strolled through their arboretum
I look up at a new commotion, not the usual
blackbirds psalming from the unleaved branches
above the Thames skiffs but among the needles
of immigrant pine and cedar, squabbling
frolicking, raucous, unafraid of the traffic
of human and dog below, jungly brilliant
not on screen or glossy page, but daubed in emerald
and ruby-beaked against the bottle-green spines
ganging together as incomers do, 'Taking over'
the natives squawk, 'our nesting sites, our grubs
berries, handouts of broken bread, our space
drowning our drab, muted calls
with their un-neighbourly din'.

HAYWAIN

Hey Wayne, your combine blocks the narrow lane
mindless of us behind, below.
I think of Cynddylan, a poet made
monarch of all he surveyed while the birds fell silent.
And Stubbs' girls, their cheeks whipped
red by June sun and wind under their bonnets
with wooden rake and fork turning
and pitching, and a smart word for the steward
or even their squire if he dared by.

You're trailing your shark's-tooth tines fitter for war
than harvest. For this is hay time again
or silage filling the silos. The fields and sheep are shorn.
Instead of stooks, drum bales stand about, plastic
sheathed in the minimalist style.
One behemoth cuts the field in half an hour
that Hopkins' Dobbin furrowed slow all day.

The cheeky girls and men posed for the painter
our taste saddles with the elegant racers
their masters owned. Yet still his haymakers
banter from the half-mown field
beside the Constable wagon. Wayne
up there on high, hooked on his lone music
no longer shares their descanting ensemble.

SATURDAY, FLYING WESTWARD

On the screen ahead the winged icon charts our flight.
It weaves across brown mountains, green plains
carrying me home. Time to switch my watch back.
The battered heart that's Africa falls away to left.
Asia looms right. Now Charlemagne's capital
swims underneath our wings. At thirty thousand feet
the headwind tries to blow us back again. Our earth
flies by below at five hundred miles an hour
and soon I can see the channel strait, that rite of passage
entrance to Hades or the gate of pleasure.
A world away it seemed with cares shrugged off
now homeward bound. London by night, garlanded
swagged by stars, by day's dun with toytown roofs
and scrubby fields. The headwind drops as we draw near
as if it knows it can't hold back our flight.
Our shadow runs before along the Thames
and we begin our harsh descent through cloudy rifts to earth.

MIROIR DE L'HOMME

The poet sees himself in 'the wondrous mirror'

Too old now for love he sees, staring in Venus' looking glass
though blind as Homer or Tiresias: the heart
the withered heart, that tin can tied to the dog's tail
(old images return) though maybe passion plagues it still
for twenty more years, unwearied as a wild swan at Coole.

Like Banquo's ghosts I see them lining up, my old haunters:
La Belle Heaulmière, Hitomaro, England's
dapper poet son. 'Not yet!' I cried, 'not yet,'
a lifetime ago. Yet now I cry again, 'Not yet.
My bloody heart still beats.'

OBIT

H.P.

'They never learn,' you said, looking back
down your century of years.
'We shot to maim not kill, aimed at their legs.'

Our generals would have shot you too
against a wall, the blindfold on, no chance
that squad would miss. You had a pact
among the lads. You knew the enemy were men
like you of bone and blood, that die.

They couldn't know of course, would've scythed
you down from their machine gun nests, and did.
Yet still we have the legend of football and fags
on Christmas Day, and carols instead of shells
across the snows of no man's land. Years on
and you both shook hands, those who had hands
to shake. Your voice speaks now from the grave
'All war's a waste.' Will we never learn?

'THAT TIME OF YEAR THOU MAYST IN ME BEHOLD . . .'

Poets don't grow old gracefully:
recall old lusts with Hardy
or clamour like Yeats for new.

'How are you?' people ask them, meaning:
'Goodness, you're still alive.'
'Are you still writing?' signals
'If so you're quite forgotten.
I haven't seen any reviews,'
and 'Aren't you going gently yet
into your goodnight?'

Gower his loins frozen by Venus
piped of a king and his bounty of wine.
Did he who'd sung of every turn and twist
of love regret the arrow's sting he'd begged
Love's priest to tear from his heart
as he lay apart from his chaste wife.
Merlin the magus besotted in old age
entombed in the rock by Nimue for his lust
must have been a poet too.
How else could he have cast such spells?

When David was old they brought him a virgin
hoping for a new Song of Solomon.
Help us all then Lady, Sappho's own goddess
to sing your song until the last bittersweet note.

ADDRESS BOOK

They come at me every year at this time
off the pages of my address book
my largely secular saints, the ones I no longer
can send carefully handpicked cards to
faces and voices I haven't the heart
or something, even to cross out. The book's
falling to pieces, held together now
with a rubber band, and by that same token
love token, when I should buy another
enter only the current, living, my hand
draws back, like a Christian commanded
to put a pinch of incense on the emperor's altar
an image out of secular Shaw, I know.
I did say unsanctified saints. But in
the old world of falling night and frost
this was the time to wake the dying sun
the dead earth. So I invoke my lost ones
off these pages, tattered, battered by years
and tears, but with their living names still.

THE DEVIL AND ALL HIS WORKS

Satan claimed me at twelve. Not witchcrafted in
but magicked all the same, by Milton.
I was him. Or he was me. To be weak
was miserable. I would be tough guy, tomboy.
Flawed angels would answer my call, be part
of my gang. There were those others who
                                        walked
in Eden with the world at their feet.
His favourites but they'd pay the price
for knowledge while I was a know-all
my family declared, outsider, outcast
bastard, 'one of those' a schoolfriend said.
So 'not to know me' would be my motto
'argues yourself unknown'. I would bestride
Hell's burning marl with him but in words
thick as those Vallambrosial leaves
if not as bright, while those others turned out
to till and toil behind counters, in offices
even 'at the mill with slaves', lost paradise
in the everyday grind. 'Pride comes before a
                                        fall,'
my aunt predicted but 'Better to reign in Hell
than serve in Heaven,' I'd think, not daring
to answer back, and then she'd add: 'It's just
difference for difference sake with you.'
While I, superior fiend, swung my school
satchel through the opening door under
an angel's sword that has barred me from
                                turning back.

THE COURSE OF TRUE LOVE . . .

Par for the course that lovers were put to the test.
Psyche sorting seeds had to call in insect labour.
Jacob served seven years for Rachel's hand.
You'd walk always on knives if you dared, swap
your mermaid tail for legs and step ashore
to follow your prince, and given the choice
of three which casket held your lady's heart
or at least her picture, and which your head
while Diarmait must kill the Fomor for denying
Grainne the sweet red rowan fruit. When
the fen fiend came stalking those who risked
being happy in hall with song and wine
they dared not lie down with their dear
companions. Awaiting her lover
Penelope wove and unpicked her shroud.

These tales, love, teach us patience in absence.
The golden box doesn't hold what money
can't buy and the monster on the dark stair
is just a childhood nightmare to be faced down.
So lovers must wait out these absent days
knowing they walk in deep-trod footprints
and only love can unpick the shroud about the heart.

USES OF A CLASSICAL EDUCATION

Narcissus is up the gym three nights a week.
Out on a binge Ariadne fell for the prettiest
boy in the rout who dumped her later.
Ganymede's been swept off his feet again
and by the villa pool Daphne shrivels
under the sun. Callisto pregnant on IVF
goes around like a bear with a sore head.
But let me still be your all encompassing cloud
your shower of gold or just carry you away in my arms.

PORTRAIT

It was part of the deal for mistress or wife
to be the muse with flesh at hand to paint
or breast or lips to sing. We know their names
often as well as those of their old masters:
Beatrice, Lisa del Giacondo, La Gouloue.
And yet who gave, who took in this so loving
barter? She looks out from her canvas shelter
or page where she might be imprisoned
set in paint or print. But no; she steps always
towards us out of the frame that would hold her.
Did you know standing with brush or pen
poised, her form flush before you, master
she was the icon we would all hanker after?

THE NEW METAPHYSIC

Corpus callosum: carapace shielding the soft body
substance, person, mass, flesh of brain-lines humming
from left to right or rather right to left, love
and reason, her to him and him to her, new science says.

The blackbird in my garden's left eye's agog
for hawk or cat while the right flutters over food
or nest. Headlit rabbits rightly freeze, while startled
ducks squawk into left-brained flight. So mind and heart

the old dichotomy still holds. Only soft lips
and eyes, hard hands conjoined can bridge our heart's abyss.
Body once chastened by the harsh and fearful soul's
our emissary now, ambassador to love's court

to plead our cause. So absence is limbo time
but not to dance; presence a haven where these
opposites meet like land and water, and corpus
callosum lays down its loving link to make us whole.

LATE STYLE

Home from sea after seven long years the sailor
takes the half token from his pocket hoping
to match it to hers still. 'The top brick off
the chimney he'd have give her,' but what would she
have done with it, heavy, rancid with soot
smirching her hands and clothes?

This year the trees are late putting on leaf, still
barely unfurled and May nearly upon them.
Yet some with a gush of bud and blossom
make up time before a summer drought dusts them
down, burst, short lived almost livid with life.
Late style should be stately, pared, tinged with to come.
Yet I go down this road swagger as a sailor
with half a ring in my pocket as if
there was no tomorrow.

FIGURINE

Surely they must have told stories or sung them
to those thin flutes of griffin bone or ivory tusk
our ancestors, the first comers as soon as the ice
drew back, that we de-humanise as cro-magnon
paleo, Gravettian, sapiens
but only just. They must have danced in those Northern
clearings they made with their flint choppers
knap, knap, knapping down to the blade
drew bison, bear, horses with their fine burins
whittled patterns on antler rods and then
took clay or jet or ochred stone to mould
or carve into those confluent breasts, belly
buttock, full labials, yet small enough
to cup in a hand, as a hand cups
a loved breast in worship, wordlessly.

SUB SPECIE

Was there no time in Eden apart from
the rising and setting of sun and moon?
No tic toc of minutes and hours breaking
the resistless flow of the day. If so
it was what we know here in each other's
arms where time stands still yet runs so fast
towards the knell of parting that we can't
stay it with kisses. Yet time will bring us
here again where there is nothing but your eyes
and mine looking love into each other
as Donne saw four hundred years ago
resting in that moment, become eternal
as we do now. Yet still warm flesh.

SLUGGISH

Ghostly gasteropod why do you graze
my carpet at night so that I find
your tracks, glinting silver in the morning
and scrub them out with the sole of my shoe?
What can you scavenge on hoovered wool
to sustain that soft muscle of a body
belly on a foot, two eyes starting out of
your jellied head with not even a shell house
to hide it in? Maybe you're on a quest, hope
a sallying forth as your trail weaves
its intricate patterns, Pollock by a footprint
continuous as Lindisfarne's interlace
or Caliphate tracery, but without
their symmetry, drunken meanderings.

Some naturalist could tell me what you're after –
Romany of my childhood who took us
unseeing on radio hunts, or perhaps
I invest you with too human a purpose
or so we think, forgetting in our hominid
hubris the first purpose is survival
and then immortality, by sex through flesh
or art. So maybe all you're looking for
is your androgynous love to come out
from under the far skirting, to meet
mid-carpet in a slithery embrace
and I, your questing fellow, though a believer
in our superiority should let you love
or at least couple and just go on scrubbing out
your love tracks in the silvering daylight.

ELEGY

I have murdered a lover. Coming home late
I cross the room in the dark to switch on
the light. Nothing alerts me, no walnut crunch
cry, underfoot squelch but when I turn
all that remains is your crushed corpse bleeding
white slime into the carpet. Next night nothing.
No telltale trail in the morning. A brooding
absence. But then today I see meandering
a silver track but only one, no
coupling snot-pool where you lay side by side.
I should rejoice I suppose. Green shoots
succulent, my plantings, safer but I
have diminished the biosphere by a byte
a jot, a nothing, aware that every day
shrinks species, tongues, the gene pools drain.
Last night in the gardens Keats knew we heard
no nightingale but saw, after rain
after drought, a colony of snails creep
onto the new sprung lawns that surround
the sad portraits, death mask of you who hymned
small things: a choir of gnats, a limping hare
a fly upon a rose, the sipping bee.

Can you the survivor grieve from the bottom
of your ganglion? Soft god of slugs
and snails, Vishnu Lord of all Life, don't send
avenging armies to strip my garden bare.
Be kind. I'm penitent. I have put out a speck
of life. I have murdered another lover.

FONTVIVE

for Jonathan and Anne

Well lady was this your spring, whatever name
we called you by, Celt, Frank, Cistercian
sprinkling you with your own waters that bubble
through a soup of silt yet are rinsed clear, as lovers'
eyes, clouded by desire, are cleansed by kissing? Once
clothes were washed where your flow gathers in cistern
and tank and now a svelte fish swims, before the stream
culverts nature's milk to plant and tree and flower.

And here I come with my votive offerings
of words and longing, praying that love will flow
as it does here down to some all nurturing lake
and you still bend above your waters, Lakshmi
Venus, Mary, whatever name we call you by.

AT THE WELCOME

Marsyas dogs us with his skin about his knees
presumptuous fluting against Apollo's lyre
believing Athena would inspire her discarded
pipe whose silver bole hadn't mirrored her face
kindly enough. (Even wisdom can sit down
with vanity.) The jury, rigged with the god's
nine golden girls, gave him the thumbs-down for
                                    his cheek.
So poets must go about the world as Woolf said
flayed. Today seeing the musculature strung out
as underskin map, or freighted vessels carrying
carmine bloodlines, innards, bony internal
carapace, I'm glad of skin masking mortality:
your smooth pelt supplely stroking mine as we lie
together, mine yours, or tacky with living sweat.

There will be time enough for pared bone as poets
know who try to clothe it in a weft of words:
love's epiderm for all who live and breathe.

TRAVELLERS

for Elaine Feinstein

Here I have followed your footprints across the world's
cities hearing your voice distinctive in every one.
Some I know, many I have only seen on maps;
poetic ambulant charting not just our orb
like globetrotting Elizabethan discoverers
Grand Tourists or your migrant forebears and mine
yours from old Odessa, mine two-sided: Fomors
from Iberia and Frenchified Vikings, neither
renowned for building cities like this London
we both love, foster mother to all comers
we would have her open her gates to in welcome
as you celebrate in her many faces, facets.
Tracking down loves, loss, voyaging light through stories
pasts, encounters, tongues, lives, time and space;
you're a traveller with no need for hardware
just your words will get us there. And so I wish
you all the time in the world to voyage on
and back; your unique voice to wormhole into
the future so that those coming after can glimpse
what it was truly like then, there and now.

PERFECTION

If I sang creation, herding words
with no angel guide except these computer
utterances telling us how it all began
spiralling down aeons to our hands held
from mere clouds of gas, some thinner
some thicker, obeying the dictum
'Perfection doesn't exist,' so that
gravity pulled the densest, heaviest
together, pushed the puny apart, making
distance, hydrogen, heat, light, stars
would I have discovered the first law
of love's physics, a force as strong
as gravity that drew us together, thinning
the world around us , until we collided
elaborating this new metaphysic, except
that in your arms that other first law
doesn't apply: 'Perfection exists'?

IN ST PAUL'S – FOR JACK DONNE

You were saved from the flames that burnt half
our city where some would have preferred
to see you perish. Supreme metaphysical, clad in
your shroud, courtesy of the sculptor
the effigy you posed for in your dying days
standing upright as if about to lift off for heaven
you would have approved Wren's telescope
high in the dome you never looked up to.

But your saved icon is ghostly, unfleshed
no lover in your grave clothes. Age and loss
pared you down to chastity. After Anne
was undone by that 'mast of children dropped
every year', fruits of your loving, and that dark
night of grief , you turned your gaze on your god
growing more dean than profane lover
but still your words burn brave, centuries
before their time and I can only try in this
half-hearted age to tread after, lame-footed
trusting you will forgive me for her sake
if I don't follow down that chaste path but still
seek my salvation in warm welcoming arms.

LARK ASCENDING: FOR R.V.W

I see you now, the sculptural head a ship's prow
breasting the sea of upturned faces as you
bore down the aisle with alms for your beloved
English songs that lingered indelibly
in your notes, lessons from Bruch and Ravel
in Berlin and Paris couldn't expel. We
painted you in the muted tones of our landscape
yet I hear in your lark's song the terror and blood
of our century, yours and mine. What would you hymn now?
What lyrics could you find to set: the woods sold off
the lark's lost nesting ground stubbled, ploughed
harrowed, nowhere to climb its ascending scale;
and London no land of Cockaigne where jobless
spectre youth kips down in doorways, cons for crack
a scenario Villon painted fit for gallows humour.

You learnt this diminishing mode in ambulance
and trench, from the drone of doodlebugs. Your
                                    music
flows like tears, and we follow its lucent streams
in hope that it can still raise us from stubble
and harrowing and our bird ascend again
flighting upscale, heralding a new spring.

CITS

This morning in the snow, old-penny-sized splodges
against the white, neat, round prints, inspecting
my rubbish sack of recyclable paper and bottles
telltale tracks the dustmen trample away
cat, or fox, maybe the one glimpsed mid-street
under the Michaelmas moon when his coughed bark
woke me, brought me to the window, squatting
to shout his defiance, big as an alsatian
and when he rose, turned to lope off, showed a brush
thick and long as a horsetail silvered by moonlight.

These lives, theirs outside, ours indoors, the hunched
pigeons on the fence, heads sunk in their chests
for warmth, waiting for bread, for me the provider
to crumble stale crusts; whose world is it? Or both,
warp and woof of our city tapestry or carpet page
where bird and animal climb the branched margins
or interlace gilded capitals while saint and squire
act out their stories for all seasons, leaving
their inked and painted prints, tales for time to retell.

PIGEON DANCING

'You're wasting your time lad,' I try to tell him.
'She doesn't want to know.' But still he dances
bows, pirouettes, teeters on window ledge
coping, burbles protestations, puffs out
his chest while she pecks at a stray feather
an invisible crumb, takes flight, flirting
or bored. Poor fool you flutter after, heart
in your crop. 'Will she, does she mean it?'
the flight or the sidelong glance that quickened
your step to an avian samba, displaying
unsure of your welcome as any lover
who daren't take our loving for granted.

THE BOOK OF THE DEAD

We have come to peer at the dead, spiced up
eviscerated, parcelled out in canopic jars
embalmed, bound, their rites of passage
painted on coffin wood, inside as well
as out before the last lid is hammered home
so they can follow correct etiquette
instructions on papyrus, plaster, shawl.

Their mouths are adzed open so the fluttering
Ba spirit can come and go. Did it hover
hawk or humming bird chirruping to come in?
And then the final lid, sculptural, pared
down to anonymity, sealed. So the Ba bird
must have passed, like neutrinos, singing
winging through matter. Last the boat, older
than Charon, crossing the dark waters
before the gates you must gain with your passport
spells, till, standing before the immortals
your heart hangs heavy from the scales weighing
good against bad. O love when they weigh
our hearts, whatever the judges, time
or tongues, let the scale tip that we loved.

NOWADAYS (T. H.)

You would have compassion for the bewildered
white bear staring out adrift on a crumbling floe
or the mother nudging her flailing cub
through freezing straits towards the nearest icefall
as you once watched that furtive hedgehog
negotiate your lawn at dusk knowing
you couldn't protect it but leaving your will
in words; all that we scribblers can do.

So this is how we looked through his lens
and would for the next quarter of a century
through Depression and war, the great unwashed;
grubby in cut-down trousers and skirts, cheap socks
wrinkling our ankles, before the shutter clicked:
aliens, a race apart from voguish portraits
glamour girls, self-seeking politicians, the writers
who could have told our story but mostly didn't.

We looked up at him, or out, nervously smiling
sooty blacked-up miners, nigger minstrels
from underground, urchins who would die
under African sun, busmen supping teabreaks
washerwomen stooped over their tubs or grinding
out sodden sheets with a heavy mangling wheel.
And I can hear their voices in chat or song
in memory's fine-tuned ear before the words
were cleansed, couthed, homogenised, gone down
in history: 'bramah, backchats, burgoo
weevil costyn, backsheesh, dough, oddmedods
boosicky, flodge . . .', coinings from base metal into gold.

TILLYA TEPE

Wearing their wealth the wandering wives
'princesses' the catalogue calls them, 'high
status' anyway, were always poised to pack up
and go, fitting their folding crowns of
buttery Bactrian gold, panned from Oxus'
clear stream, into saddlebags, or safe on
their backs, sequined friezes sewn into seams
as refugees have always carried their hopes
from past or for future to present exile
while their lord, princeling of Kushan, shot
Parthian style over his horse's rump
as they fled across Alexander's furthest
reaches of empire until, wars ended, at last
they could make it their own, bartering silks
and spices to travel their high peaked passes.

Those girls, were their cheeks flushed russet
like the Usbek daughters I saw brought
by their mothers to rub the dust from
the tombs of Tamerlane's womenfolk across
their plump cheeks for fertility or to
ward off an evil eye, and still wearing
the bright coloured robes we see the gilt
trappings of, laid out in the ghostly
finery sketching these graves. Latecomers
to this land, after Persian, Greek, Roman
but before Arab or the *Boys' Own* heroes
playing out their Great Kipling Games
on the roof of the world, you inherited
Dionysus' wine cup, Aphrodite's stone
folds of carved chiton, bearded gold bulls
from the Tigris, glass goblets brought from Rome
a China bowl, an Indian statuette
to this high delta of riverine roads.

Like Cuthbert's bones the monks caught up and carried
fleeing fire to Durham, their guardians hid
these testaments to their rich past, now brought
out here for our eyes, distanced by space and time
to gaze on, away from looters, that old trade
and our bloodier century's fire, to make again
that brief Bactrian calm in these relics
where all roads meet telling our human story.

Going back… Are we always going back because
to go on is to the end? I took you back to
my beginnings on a day of sun and blossom
green lawns where nuns once walked, finding the street
the house, still there. 'Go to the door Madgie, it's them!'
when we did the family rat-a-tat-tat-a-tat.
But we had always been going back, the home
in the heart being where it is, through unloved
backchats beside 'the works', like thousands before us
exiles, wanderers with no place to call our own
except in memory. In the front garden, a panel
of concrete before the street, now a discarded
armchair moulders. A hummock of grass has pushed out
the next turning where Aunt Marion, once backrow
in our local Tiller Girls line-up, lived
with Cousin Jack, and fake rural names of nut trees
hazel, pine and walnut, have displaced the Essex
legacy of our past when great-grandfather
economic migrant from his countryside's
collapse, came down the line from Thaxted to shoe
the dray horses in the railway yards to this selfsame
street of workers' cottages like those they'd left behind
no bathroom, an outdoor lavatory still when I came back
to live, eighty years later. My great-grandparents stare
out of their portrait taken in a Stratford studio
nervously defiant, 'as good as the next'.
Now the back bedroom where I slept should sport a bath
with a lavatory under the stairs where we kept
the coal, that gave off a methane reek on hot days.
Do they keep chickens, grow tomatoes
in the back garden? What's become of the
Anderson shelter? I want to ring the new bell
but know all going back's a loss. Only the long

hard stare of history can make sense of these
unwritten, unacknowledged lives; yet they were.

The house stands as it did but I feel nothing.
It was where we always came back to after
myriad others (once I counted up more homes
than years), not ours but it was home. Even when
the sky was aflame with fire, in the thump of bombs
and we crouched holidaying in that shelter while
my father-uncle watched from the entrance as if
standing still on the firestep of his trench twenty odd
years before or calmer days' trips to plays and shows, until
I came to finish my schooling there and all my world
changed again. Now I write this towards the end
though not quite yet I hope. Poets should go down
satirical or brave, preferably young like
Keats and Shelley, romantic duo. Until I was
seventeen I thought I would follow them out
watery grave or coughing up my lungs like
my mother and John's, him too, who'd choked in their own
blood, and wasn't I a regular at Plaistow
chest clinic? Yet here I am dancing on the shore
in love as if for the first time. 'There's no fool like
an old fool.' Maybe, but now we live on
they must let us love. So back to the past
to the house where the daddy-long-legs lurked
in the lavatory above the cistern and in summer
sunlight streamed over the top of the door
from the garden beyond, where the bath was under
boards in the kitchen beside the copper you had
to light, but only once a week, with paper
and sticks, and coal. How can a lifetime encompass
so much? I turn the tap on and the water runs hot.

When those Britons felt the first warmth of a Roman
hypocaust under their feet did they think: 'I want
one of those and a smart new villa, mosaic floors
painted walls and all'? And there it will be
in the photographs you took and my words
this street that partied the end of a war, coronations
Mum Kirby's golden wedding ('Fancy being married
to that miserable old sod for sixty years!'
my aunt said as she beat the eggwhite and sugar
into icing on the cake), somewhere not eclipsed
by time and the planner's heavy hand.

What marks a memory out to become a bright bead
on the strung lifeline like the marbles, glinting
or muddied, we chased down the gutters, our currency
for swapping or conkers with their brownshoe polish?
This year summer has come in April, the year draining
away while I would linger it out not knowing what
the next may bring of loss. Flowers burst as soon
as bud, bees viking in the weigela honeying home
to masonry hives. Hover-flies dry their gelatine
wings on foxglove leaves grown soft on sunlight

My skin sheds scurf of spent cells. We die from outside
inward like some fallen monument time weathers
to dust. 'Always keep the best till last,' the old saw
said and so I do, leaving the coffee cream the final
toothful in the box, the last mouthful of toast with
its cargo of buttery poached yolk, the mushroomed
pizza heart. But how to know when's last, what's best?
Missing the one you might tumble into the other
that's nothingness. So I relish each moment, not
knowing what's to come as the year unreels

its torrent of blossom and bees and the petals
of pale montana confetti down while thunder
rolls across the sunlit sky presaging downpour.

I remember in Livy's *History of Rome*
our setbook for the second test (the first
we'd taken at ten) we'd have to pass to go on
and up, as we thought or were led to believe
his doubts: 'And if I should start and tell the tale
from the beginning…should I have done a worthwhile
thing?' as we clumsily translated, and I can doubt
the attempt to pick up on just one life
like the hovering fairground tongs that always
let slip the coveted prize as it swung towards you
let alone a whole people's story. And wouldn't it
take as long again, another lifetime, unless
the censoring memory itself had whittled
away, leaving often just the seemingly trivial
we treasure: shells pebble fretted or lime washed
bleached by the waves, flawed glass gems from bottles
shorn of their messages, water worn, empty whelk
egg cases, whitened cuttlebone, remnants, cast aways
yet still holding the sussuration or smell of the sea
that tossed them up out of its unfathomed maw.

Do we learn or just go on because we must? Art
doesn't progress, building brick on brick. It merely
chameleons with time and place, history and
geography of the mind and heart, those old
ragbag clichés of metaphor we dust off
and cut to fit our present need. I box up
my archive, my writing life. Do I feel bereft
seeing it vanning away to its hope of an

afterlife? 'We will be remembered in our songs,'
Sappho promised and Behn begged for her verses'
immortality. These children grow up and fly away
on paper wings or cruise like Milton's fallen angels
through the ether, and I rarely visit unless asked.
Is it birthing or fostering, surrogate from those
who've gone before, then the hope to fertilise
be seminal ourselves, hubris or just bowing
to some urge to pass on the mind's genes, echoing
what winds the rest of nature's clockwork?

Life writing, the writing life, and both perhaps
just a 'howling in the dark' as Yeats said
while I, still greedy, demanding more, hunger too
for that 'perfection of the life' I find on your lips
in your arms as we perfect our own lovechild.

TOOLS

My uncle Jack of all trades brought back from France
the candlesticks he'd crafted from German shell-
cases that grace my table, and carpentered
from mahogany off-cuts the little box
harbouring my spare fuses, whose lid sockets
perfectly into its brown body. Now I have
his tools: whetstone, box plane, chisel and the pocket
set he carried: bradawl, gimlet, screwdriver
in their leather case stamped, 'Handyman', with
the arms of Scarborough town, picked up
on some seaside holiday. But not
those others: trenching iron, flogging hammer
and the 'pom-pom' that deadened his bloodless fingers
as he punched out the guts of old steam boilers
filling his gas-tattered lungs with soot till
he spat black phlegm into the kitchen sink.

Today seeing the rack of ancient tools
old gardeners sweated over, hand crafted
I can see his hands, pocked with shrapnel stains
yet delicate to pick out a hair-fine
herring bone or finger a blade for sharpness
before he stropped it on the moistened whetstone
darkened wet slate, penknife or spade, honed
to carve or slice London dirt, or weld
at work with soldering iron, spirits of salt
and molten silver, the colour of his hair.

LEX INNOCENTIS 697

When Adomnan laid down his law, calling together
the princes and the warriors, that the deaths
of civilians, women and children, non-combatants
should be paid for in blood money, wergild
(compensation our half-hearted word) the law
of the innocent in that seventh century we dub
the Dark Ages, he appointed guardians
overseers to make it stick. So when my aunt
my mother's sister was killed by a stray Nazi
bomb she'd have had a hide of land, a couple
of goats, her weight in gold, by rights, in those
barbarous times. And the thousands now in our
civilised century brought out from rubbished homes
laid in mute rows like bundles of old carpet
some longer, some childishly small, what should
their price be, beyond the dreams of avarice?
Only these bitter fruit, enough to make a saint weep.

TECHNOLITHIC

The nurse pops a cake-icer into my ear.
The sharp ping tells her I'm not burning up.
And now I have seen it all: flint, obsidian
horn, bronze, iron. Once a white-capped
sister placed a glass phial carefully under
my tongue, a poison pen of mercury
held my wrist, counting while the watch pinned
to her domed, blue bosom ticked my pulse away.
Now Ayala from Bangalore loops my arm
To her robot, checking me in or out.
Only the clip-board and pen survive
the half century, noting my blood's tides.

LATE SONG

'Young enough to be his daughter,' the tongues
would have tut-tutted, 'granddaughter even!'
But their eyes had met across their common love
his arm raised keeping time, her hair sweeping
the straight bow letting fly their cupid's arrow.
Music carried them away, a dream not just
of the soul but of the flesh. Just a couple of years
of bliss, of common time, shared staves yet
the notes flowed again, andante, scherzo
unseemly still harmonious, 'her theme'
a portrait in sound as a brush might have
captured the loved contours, instead a quartet
songs, another symphony he knew he might never
finish, her melody a stranger would embody
sixty years later. And yet he must have hoped
their song would be unending, a 'first sketch'
for lovers everywhere, in that land where corals lie.

SMILE

'So I can discharge you from this clinic,'
the young Spanish doctor smiles. Reprieved then
free to shoot off. Not wanted here. Dazed
winding back through the scrubbed corridors
I'm suddenly stopped by a trickle of notes.
At first I don't see beside the space where
patients and visitors can pretend to café
culture, egg and chips, burgers, diet coke
angel cake, the back of a head, white
knobtailed, male or female, but the waltzing song
I recognise from childhood draws me towards
the upright piano, the deft fingers
exacting the tune. I dare to go near. Up close
spectacles and white-stubbled chin define him.

'I think you must have been a professional,'
I offer, remembering an aunt who played
in the silent picture palaces. He smiles up
at me. 'No. Do you play?' 'No.' 'Sing?'
'I used to. Not any more.' But his hands
fluttering across the keys are bringing
another memory of family sing-songs.
I begin to mouth the words lying intact
in their cave of the past: 'Sweetheart!'
They jostle forward to take their bow
against the clatter of cutlery, dishes
and I see smiling up at us a lone diner
momentary audience among the scrubbed
corridors, consulting rooms, wards
theatres of life and death. I thank him
for us all but already as I turn away
 'Always' begins to flower under
his hands while I descend out through
'Reception' into the smiling street.

THISTLEDOWN

It was easy when I was a kid: you
only had to get to the end of the path
above the railway embankment
and the Great Western trains thundering
through below, before the gate clanged to
behind you, and everything would be alright;
the only imponderable could you
run fast enough. Later there were daisy petals
to help you decide, dandelion clocks
for telling when it was home time and Black
Cat cigarette packets you had to stamp on
for good luck. Then with the years the imponderables
came to sit in an accusing row chanting
'What about us?' The dandelion clock
blew away in a puff of thistledown
and the white petals couldn't tell me
anymore the answer to that eternal question
the only 'yes' or 'no' that really matters.

ROMANTICS

How you might have loved this sight: the sublime
mountain a white cliff, three sisters still shining
above the lake though the shore steeps are ribbed
with gleaming villas that throw back the sun
until they meet the glossy city, high tenements
to commerce, mammon heights you could never
have imagined. In your day the other was foetid
London alleys where men heard only
each others' groan, not this slap of water
where golden girls and boys frolic their perfect
limbs, a coot dips her white nasal and there skims
a waterskier in the creamed wake of a launch.

Now you might weep rather for lost purity
innocence of mountains and water, in
bankerland, your dream sullied with money's
sweaty prints that hold our world to ransom.

Only that for a moment on the low parapet
that walls the water in a fledgling sparrow
bullies a parent to be fed, ubiquitous or
decamped from London planes. Small lives
go on in the corporate interstices
scrubby foxtail grasses seed themselves
a canopy of carrion gulls underpins the sky
while a butterfly beats white wings against
the breeze as an ant scales my shirt and the mountains
shimmer and melt beneath the blue lens above.

FOUNDLINGS

These were the ones that were found, and found a place
not left to founder on cold stone doorstep, choke
on a rubbish dump or drowned like kittens in a sack.
Here I could have ended up then, if I'd been
lucky, wetnursed out to suck in goodness
that might have saved me against the brutal chance
of one in five killed off, even of these rescued
their identities like those of evacuees tied
to wrist or neck, bracelet, coral necklace or just
a button, coin or note if mum could write, or find
a friend who could, in hope they'd be back to claim
happy ever after. But my mother wouldn't have
made it. Not that she was one for Hogarth's Gin Lane
patron with Handel and Dickens, supporting these
discarded. More like his young girl, love betrayed
one hand on her belly, the other clutching at
the arm of the soldier marching away. She always
came back from some sanatorium bed to claim me.
But then, no, not then: a single mum in eighteenth-
century Slum Lane, unwed, hacking her lungs out.

Some of them made it into apprenticeships or
as powder monkeys, buglers, the boys already
uniformed, the girls aproned into service.
One mother, elegantly clad, gloved and gowned
almost a lady, come, hoping to take back
the baby she'd left, got only the death certificate.
Yet most of us did better than at home, pricked
against smallpox, gruel or milk porridge for
breakfast when it wasn't just bread, as much
or more than my mother who had to share the top
of father's egg or tail of his bloater with her
siblings or the sop from the milky dregs of mother's
tea with crumbled bread and a sprinkle of sugar.

It was a little world watered with women's tears
of mothers handing over the swaddled bundles
or nurses weeping when they had to send them back.
while the foundling father slipped away scot-free.
And we had to be healthy bastards to have the chance
of a place, or win the lottery of tumbling balls.
But one who never came back for James or John
in her terror she couldn't remember his short-
lived name, but pleaded in a letter from Newgate's
death-row for him to be taken in, never knew
whether they threw him back with his tainted blood
to die, cutpurse or dipper, like his mother, swinging
from the gibbet or kitted him out in blue fustian
to perish with Nelson in *Victory*'s hold.

MARGINAL GLOSSES

I

EXETER 31

That old riddler of Exeter 31 when the woman
heard him from where she stood half-hidden
behind the hangings, did she think: 'That's me
a pipe he can play on with gold rings
round my neck where my jealous brothers
hang. I see him look towards me as he sings
but he's only a wandering wordsmith
here for the free beer the king's lady
offers him in the golden goblet. Even his pipe's
not his own. It's passed from hand to hand
but that's not me. His eyes seek me out
as his fingers hover over the chanter
and I grow limp as the hanging birdfoot
that speaks my desire, webbed as a waterfowl's
paddle. And I would be held close under his arm
and yes I will sing for him, believing, believing.'

II

ENVIRONMENTAL STUDIES:
CUTHBERT AND THE ANIMALS

Miracles of bird or beast: on a bleak
yet beautiful strand the saint walks into the sea
up to his neck in the cold salt waves, praying
to his god who walked on water or Neptune
who ruled the waves. Is he joining ancient
and modern, classic, fairy, Christian or just
calling on that other who moved upon

the face of the deep summoning order out
of chaos? Now we can make our own parable
from those generous beasts who came to warm him
with their breath, sea otters from faraway
Sargasso, leaving their frolicking
in the offshore ripples for him who talked
with ravens, taught them to pray and give up
their predations on his roof straw to build
their own nests. Clever corvos, they came back
with gifts, their spokesman spreading his wings
in contrition and bowing his head, before they
dumped the pig's fat stolen from somewhere
at his feet as tribute for pilgrims to grease
their shoes. And the sleek otters who came ashore
to dry him with their fur, rubbing against
chilled legs and belly so he could join
the others at service while they slipped
away back into their watery zones
do they suggest Cuthbert knew even then
our world was one, living and breathing
he whose hunger was slaked by the sea eagle's
catch, the mighty fish he ordered to be cut in two
and the great bird given back its half share?

III
CENEWYF

It was tough enough for the princesses
ruling their holy domains, to get themselves
into the history books, lives of saints
chronicles. They had to set up synods
broker deals between North and South, Celt
and Roman, go missionary to barbarous lands

govern communities with all the bickering
backbiting of limited companies.
One of them even dared to be a poet
in the holiest of tongues. But where hidden
in the shadows is the rarer, rarest
girl Caedmon? Somewhere our Cenewyf
must have been scouring a pot, grubby slag
not gold adorned, sleeping like her brother
on straw in an outhouse, fending off
the gilded warriors soused with dark beer
wanting a lay that wasn't set to the harp.

Did her angel come too, gliding downy-winged
with honeyed songs, a lily outstretched or
piercing spear in a delicate hand, second
visitation as you Theresa suffered later?
So why not then? Bidding her versify
what? Creation, annunciation, marriage
to an old man, the death of a child?
Did Hild or Aethelthryth come to the barn
where she was sleeping with beasts, take her
in their arms and lead her to light, comfort
chastity, virginity but not write down
her words, knowing it was merely ecstasy
delusion, a kind of madness. So she
doesn't come at us off the poetry pages.

Still I see her bringing in a willow-
woven tray of scoured goblets and thinking
as she listened to the harp going the rounds
and the songs rang out: 'I could do that.'

IV
DRAGONSPEAK

I'll tell you how I came by it that heap
of glistening gold they stole from me.
Flying above the earth, mountain and sea
mapped out below, looking for a place
to roost or nest, I saw the cave mouth.
Not knowing of course what lay inside
went in. A gleam in the gloom from the darkest
depths under a high arched roof. No guardian
that I could sniff out or I would have thrashed
my tail and backed out as is the rule.
So I claimed it by squatter's right, and as rightful
keeper and the centuries passed.

Some nights I'd take a trip to exercise
the old flame-thrower; they clinker up
you know with disuse, burn up a few miles
of moorland while the humans shivered
beside their fires telling tall tales how the hoard
came there, left by the last prince of his people
abandoned. Typical of mankind. No
stamina. New comers, while we'd been around
for aeons before they stood up on their hind legs
after the cataclysm when dark and cold
enveloped the earth. I'm one of the last.
My mother survived, went back to the sea depths
to bear me, a single egg. I grew up
fed on fire till my time came: I was strong enough
to paddle up into the sunlight.

They'll blame me of course; humans always do.
A scorched earth policy they'll dub it
just because I torched their proud Heorot
like any herdsman's hut. But it was mine

wasn't it, guarded through ages in the place
I'd made my home till that thief, that outcast
stole in and nicked a golden goblet, hoping
to buy his way back in, appease the men
with its glitter, offer to lead them
to my treasure trove. Then I was mad
went abroad flaming on my wide wings
breathing out scorching wrath. Showed them.

So the old man boasted he'd come after me
grey hairs and all. Got himself a shield of steel
hefted his trusted grey sword, alone against me.
I'm old too but with us it doesn't count.
Centuries pass, our scales burnish to iron.
Wings strengthen, flame breath lengthens
a furnace stoked by time. He came on
to single combat, trusting in old skills
old conquests, with his ancient blade that broke
on my bone. But it bloody hurt. So I torched him.
Then up comes this lad, wanting to be a hero.
I blasted his shield down to the boss, to charcoal.
So he hides behind the old man's but when
I rush in again, fuming fire, the old
grey sword snaps in my head. I sink
my teeth in the withered neck and the boy
sticks me deep in my guts with his knife.

I feel my fire going out and the old one
takes his knife too from his belt and cuts me
in half. The indignity of it: my eyes dimming
my tail still thrashing about like a severed worm.
But he had no time to gloat. His bitten neck
swells and burns with my poisonous spittle.
The knife blade melted in my venomous blood.
Then they ransacked my gold to heap on his pyre

and me they rolled to the top of the cliff
and over into the waves boiling below.
I sank down, down, down far below to where
we once came to hatch our rubbery eggs
so the dragonlets could play at the fissures
in the earth's crust, those chimneys where boiling
magma spews out to nourish them, kindle
their first flame before they can rise through the murk
take wing. That was long ago. Now I roll
with the thrust of tides, the heave of the earth's
plates, shields locking together in the wall
or breaking, drifting apart. But remembered
by men wherever the prince's death is sung.

V

DEOR

Did your lord and master give you your name
Deor, precious poet, dear one? As another
might say now: 'You're very valuable to our list
after winning the Nobel, you know. Even though
you don't make us as much money as a failed
politician's randy memoirs,' before
he dumped you. Was it just that you were no longer
young and handsome, an ornament
to the meadhall and he fell for a new bard?
Poets have no lien on lands. Exiled, a wanderer
no longer on mainstream lists, festival
programmes, magazined, this 'craft so long
to learn' brings you your only comfort.

Poets have always known it so don't hold up
the sufferings of Weland, cuffed and bound
Beadohild's grief, Meathild unhappy in love

the peoples punished by tyrants as heartsease
while your sorecaring soul resonates down
down the centuries. We have all felt what
it is to be ousted by 'the full sail
of his proud verse' like a dear deer once
hand-fed now hounded off the land: Clare
tucked away in the Northampton asylum
after the glamoring of London's lights.

Those may have passed over, this doesn't.

VI
JUDITH

Not at all the sort you'd want to marry, more like
our Aethelflaed or her crazy daughter, Aelfwyn
getting themselves up in armour, leading men out
to fight against the Danes, and, at least the mother
winning too, though Aelfwyn went and lost it all
again. Or more like those old Welsh queens
you read about, burning down London
thrashing the Romans, barbarians beaten in the end.
Or like that Judith. Oh it has to be alright
if God himself says so but not a pattern
for our girls to follow or you wouldn't know
when you might wake up to find you'd lost
your head. He probably wasn't such a bad
chap either that Holofernes. These things
happen in war and, no doubt, he thought he deserved
some reward for leading his lot to victory
like one of us really, getting drunk after
in the mead hall with his men. But he shouldn't
have passed out. Girls don't like it.
They like to be dear bed companions

even if they're sleeping with the enemy
and she'd got that other woman with her
which is always dangerous. So when his men
brought him to the bed and drew the golden curtain
he tumbled in snoring where he couldn't be seen
and away they went to down more draughts
till they were all snoring too. So what does she do
but out with a sword, his or hers, and up and off
with his head though she had to strike twice
before it rolled to the floor. Then she hands it
to the girlfriend, cool as an ice maiden
who tucks it into the bag they'd brought
their supper in, meat and wine that had helped
get her courage up, and off they go
with their bloody trophy, the enemy warriors
still sleeping it off, the gates unguarded
back to their own camp where she holds it up.

There's a great shout and away men march
buckling on armour, grabbing sword, spear and bow
to where the Assyrians were still snoring.
Showers of arrows they let fly, rousing them
hungover from deep draughts of mead.
Waking they ran to their leader's tent
drew back the gold curtain, found him headless
lifeless. Broken they fled pursued by the heroes
hacking at the helmets, shattering shieldwalls.
Stripping the dead, they brought the golden hoard
to Judith, to lay at her feet beside Holofernes'
helmet. Sword hilts and scabbards, buckles
and mead cups, bigger than the hoard we had
to bury at Licitfelda. And the moral of all this
for all the tales have a moral: don't fall asleep
on the job, choose your girl carefully
mix more water with your mead and never
never wear your sword to bed.

VII
SEAFARING – EXETER 68, 69, 74

Ships are always she, breasting the waves
figure-heading into latitudes
water wives luring the sailors away
from land-locked lovers to drown in difference
foreign ports and parts, going Viking
northwards to meet the ice queen or south
into doldrums, sargassos, before fandango
salsa, 'mermaids of the street' sucking
you down to their salt caverns while your lovers
wait, one quayside for you to gangplank back;
one over the horizon, dockside for news.

You stumble back on board so she can plough
her liquid path, hull flecked with sea dapple
north again where the snow queen swims in seas
of ice, diamonds in her crown that the sun flashes
to fire. There they meet but not breast
to shattering breast; but one deep sounding
for that full flounced skirt of whalebone
that would rack and wreck, water become
ivory, tusked and tearing. So the ship
stands off, admiring from her distance
turns for home while she, born of water
married to frost, goes on majestic
through pack ice into sea lanes till the sun
ravishes her again to water.

Nearing the port the sailor stands on deck
hoping for the flutter of a white
handkerchief, warm flesh waiting, smooth arms
before the cold sea wife claims him back.

FRIENDS OF ENITHARMON

The following have generously become Patrons and Sponsors
of the *Friends of Enitharmon* scheme, enabling this
and other publications to come into being:

PATRONS

Duncan Forbes
Sean O'Connor
Masatsugu Ohtake
Myra Schneider

SPONSORS

Kathy & Jeff Allinson
Colin Beer
Natasha Curry
Vanessa Davis
Jack Herbert
Alison M. Houston
Sylvia Riley
Angela Sorkin
Janet Upward